SCIENCE DISCOVERY

Communication

Q & A

Janice Parker

www.av2books.com

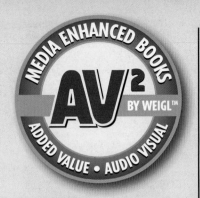

MEDIA ENHANCED BOOKS
AV²
BY WEIGL™
ADDED VALUE • AUDIO VISUAL

Go to **www.av2books.com**, and enter this book's unique code.

BOOK CODE

J 6 1 2 8 1 5

AV² by Weigl brings you media enhanced books that support active learning.

AV² provides enriched content that supplements and complements this book. Weigl's AV² books strive to create inspired learning and engage young minds in a total learning experience.

Your AV² Media Enhanced books come alive with...

Audio
Listen to sections of the book read aloud.

Video
Watch informative video clips.

Embedded Weblinks
Gain additional information for research.

Try This!
Complete activities and hands-on experiments.

Key Words
Study vocabulary, and complete a matching word activity.

Quizzes
Test your knowledge.

Slide Show
View images and captions, and prepare a presentation.

... and much, much more!

Published by AV² by Weigl
350 5ᵗʰ Avenue, 59ᵗʰ Floor
New York, NY 10118
Websites: www.av2books.com   www.weigl.com

Library of Congress Control Number: 2013953144

ISBN 978-1-4896-0680-8 (hardcover)
ISBN 978-1-4896-0681-5 (softcover)
ISBN 978-1-4896-0682-2 (single user eBook)
ISBN 978-1-4896-0683-9 (multi-user eBook)

Printed in the United States of America, in North Mankato, Minnesota
1 2 3 4 5 6 7 8 9 0 18 17 16 15 14

042014
WEP300113

Project Coordinator Aaron Carr
Designer Mandy Christiansen

Contents

What Is Communication?

Communication refers to the various ways we send and receive messages. The messages can be written words, sounds, pictures, or video. Writing email, publishing newspapers, and broadcasting television programs are just a few of the ways people communicate with one another. Science has developed new technologies that make communication easier and faster. Jobs are created as new methods of communication are invented. Today, contacting other people or receiving current news is as easy as picking up a **smartphone** or turning on a television or computer. This ease of communication helps people feel closer to others all over the world.

How Scientists Use Inquiry to Answer Questions

When scientists try to answer a question, they follow the process of scientific inquiry. They begin by making observations and asking questions. Then, they propose an answer to their question. This is called the hypothesis. The hypothesis guides scientists as they research the issue. Research can involve performing experiments or reading books on the subject. When their research is finished, scientists examine their results and review their hypothesis. Often, they discover that their hypothesis was incorrect. If this happens, they revise their hypothesis and go through the process of scientific inquiry again.

Process of Scientific Inquiry

Observation

Communication **hardware** is often used by scientists to gather and analyze information. Meteorologists are scientists who study weather. They use pictures and information sent from **satellites** to understand and forecast weather.

Have You Answered the Question?

The cycle of scientific inquiry never truly ends. Once meteorologists understand hurricanes, they may ask, "How can we better forecast tornadoes?"

Research

Meteorologists studying satellite images can see a hurricane developing over the ocean. They study other data, or information, from the satellite, such as the storm's wind speed. They may also look at data from earlier storms. They ask questions such as, "Where is the storm moving? When will it reach land?"

Results

If their forecast was wrong, meteorologists analyze the data again. They try to understand why the storm took a different course.

Hypothesis

After watching the storm's movement over a period of time, meteorologists form a hypothesis. They forecast where and when the storm will reach the coastline.

Experiment

Meteorologists continue to track, or study, the hurricane. When the storm strikes land, they find out whether their forecast was correct.

How Did Printing Improve Communication?

Thousands of years ago, speech and gestures were the only forms of communication. Stories and information were passed by word of mouth. An important change in communication happened when people began to write things down.

Ancient peoples wrote first on clay, then on **papyrus**, and finally on paper. At first, anything on paper had to be written by hand. This included whole books. To make a second copy of a book, all of the words had to be handwritten again. Few people could read, and even fewer people owned books.

▼ Johannes Gutenberg used a new kind of printing press he invented to print Bibles in Germany in the 1400s.

▲ A history of Chinese rulers was printed using wood blocks in the 11th century.

Another major change in communication took place when printing presses were invented. A printing press is a machine used to place words and pictures on paper. Printing presses allowed people to make many copies of the same words or stories.

The first printed pages were made in China. Words and pictures were carved into blocks of wood. The surface of the wood was covered with ink, and the block was pressed down on a piece of paper. By adding more ink to the wood block, many copies of the same words and pictures could be made. The first printed book was made in this way around AD 868.

Digging Deeper

Your Challenge!

Typesetting means combining letters to make entire pages of words, or text. Today, computers are used for typesetting. To dig deeper into the issue:

There are thousands of typefaces, or styles of type. Some look modern, others old-fashioned. Using a computer, type three messages. Make one to a friend, one to a family member, and one to a teacher. Then, choose a typeface you think goes best with each message.

Summary

The printing press improved communication by allowing information and stories to be shared.

Further Inquiry

Other inventions also helped communication. Maybe we should ask:

How did airplanes change the mail system?

How Did Airplanes Change the Mail System?

Compared to some new forms of communication, delivering letters by mail may seem slow to people today. However, the mail system was once much slower than it is now. At first, people had to travel many miles on foot to deliver a letter. Then, horses and other animals were used. In the mid-1800s, the Pony Express used horses to carry letters across the western United States.

The invention of trains and automobiles sped up mail delivery. Mail still took many days to travel from one place to another. When letters were carried by ships across the ocean, it could take months before they reached their destination.

The airplane was invented in the early 1900s. Soon after, planes were being used to carry "airmail." The use of airplanes changed mail delivery forever. Airmail takes only hours or a few days to travel across the country or around the world.

Even with many **electronic** forms of communication available today, airmail is still widely used. The United States Postal Service handles 160 billion pieces of mail each year. Canada Post delivers about 4 billion pieces of mail a year.

⌄ A letter mailed in Kansas on Monday may be delivered in Florida by Wednesday.

Digging Deeper

Your Challenge!

For many years, the postal system was the best way to send written and printed communication across a long distance. To dig deeper into the issue:

Mail a letter to a friend or relative in a different part of the country. Ask a parent if you can add tracking information to the letter. There is a small charge for tracking a letter. How long does the letter take to reach its destination? Where did it go along the way?

Summary

Using airplanes, the postal system can get letters and other printed materials to their destinations quickly and at low cost.

Further Inquiry

For years, electronic forms of communication have competed with the postal service. One early form of electronic communication was the telegraph. Maybe we should ask:

What is a telegraph?

What Is a Telegraph?

A telegraph is a machine that uses electricity to send and receive messages carried along wires. Telegraphs are rarely used today. However, they made communication much faster when they were invented in the 1800s. Telegraph messages are sent by turning electricity on and off. Short bursts of electric current are sent along wires to the receiving telegraph. Early telegraph receivers had magnetic needles on a dial with the letters of the alphabet written on it. Separate wires and coils acted as **electromagnets** and controlled each needle. The current from the sending machine created strong magnetic energy in the coils. As each letter was sent, the magnetic energy made a needle point to that letter on the dial.

In 1844, Samuel Morse invented a way to make it even easier and quicker to send messages by telegraph. He developed a code, later named Morse code. Each letter or number is represented by a series of dots and dashes. Dots are created by very short bursts of electricity, while dashes are created by longer bursts.

Like all telegraphs, a Morse telegraph is made up of two parts, a sender and a receiver. An operator uses a switch on the sender to tap out short or long burst of electric current. At the other end, a receiver reads the bursts as dots or dashes. The receiver prints out the message. A telegraph operator then translates the Morse code into words.

⌄ The switch on a Morse telegraph used to type the message was also sometimes called the key.

> Telegraph wires could carry messages hundreds or even thousands of miles.

Digging Deeper

Your Challenge!

The invention of Morse code made it easier to send and receive messages by telegraph. To dig deeper into the issue:

Research the Morse code symbols that stand for each letter and number. Write a short message to a friend, and then translate it into Morse code.

Summary

Telegraphs deliver messages using electricity and magnetic energy.

Further Inquiry

If electricity and magnetic energy are used in communication, maybe we should ask:

What are electromagnetic waves?

What Are Electromagnetic Waves?

Electromagnetic waves are electrical and magnetic vibrations that travel through the air. They allow messages to be sent without using wires. The discovery of electromagnetic waves in the 19th century led to a new form of communication.

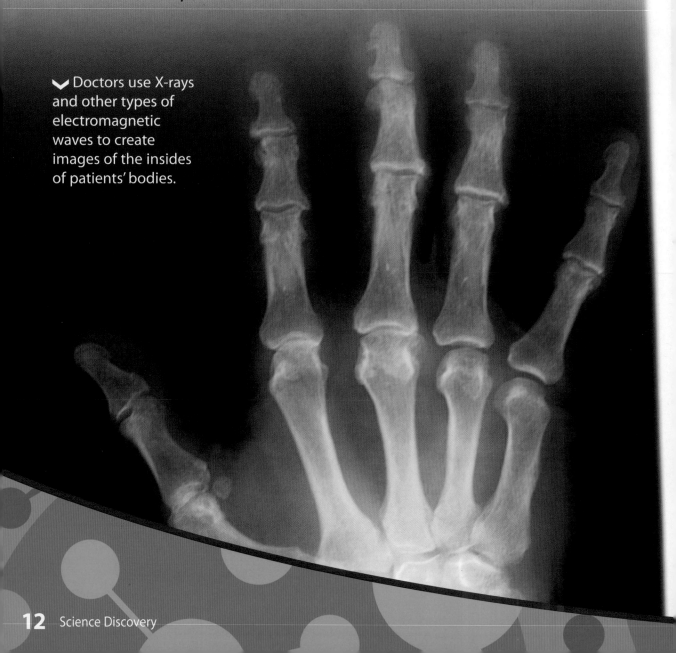

❯ Doctors use X-rays and other types of electromagnetic waves to create images of the insides of patients' bodies.

^ The microwaves used to cook or heat food are absorbed by water in the food. The waves make the water hot.

Electromagnetic waves are rays of electrical energy that exist in wave shapes. Like waves in water, electromagnetic waves have high points, called crests, and low points, called troughs. Wavelength is the length of a wave from one crest to the next. There are many different types of electromagnetic waves. Ultraviolet rays, which are part of sunlight and can cause sunburn, are one type. X-rays, microwaves, and radio waves are other types. Each type has wavelengths that are within a specific range. Radio waves have longer wavelengths than any other type of electromagnetic waves.

Radio waves can be sent over short distances. However, some can travel distances as long as 6,250 miles (10,000 kilometers). Radio waves can even travel into outer space. All radio waves travel at the speed of light. This is 186,282 miles (299,792 km) per second.

Your Challenge!

Radio waves are a type of electromagnetic waves that can be used to send messages. To dig deeper into the issue:

Research the different wavelengths that radio waves can have. List several types of communication that use radio waves of different wavelengths.

Summary

Electromagnetic waves allow messages to travel through the air without wires.

Further Inquiry

If radio waves can be sent over great distances, maybe we should ask:

What is radio?

What Is Radio?

Radio is a way to communicate by sending sounds wirelessly. These sounds may include music. They may also include human voices and other types of information.

The first radio communication signals were sent by Guglielmo Marconi in 1895. Marconi experimented with radio waves when he was a young man in Italy. He created a wireless telegraph machine that could send radio waves through the air. He was able to send messages in Morse code over distances of 2 miles (3.2 km). Marconi later created more powerful wireless telegraph equipment that could send and receive radio signals over longer distances. After Marconi moved to England, he succeeded in sending radio signals across the English Channel in 1899. Those signals traveled between France and England.

A couple of years later, Marconi sent radio signals across the Atlantic Ocean from England to eastern Canada. They traveled more than 2,000 miles (3,200 km). Other scientists did not think it was possible to send radio waves so far because Earth is round. The waves would have to curve around it. However, certain types of radio waves can bounce off a layer of Earth's atmosphere. This allows them to travel around the curve of Earth.

❯ The Eiffel Tower in Paris, built for the 1889 World's Fair, was set to be torn down in 1909. However, officials realized it was useful for sending radio signals.

Soon, radio communication was used by ships at sea. Before radio, ships could send messages to other ships only if the two vessels were in sight of one another. Such messages were often sent in code using flags or lights. With radio, ships could communicate with more distant vessels.

▼ In 1899, Guglielmo Marconi put radio equipment aboard two ships to report on progress of the America's Cup yacht race.

Digging Deeper

Your Challenge!

The ocean liner *Titanic* sent radio messages asking for help after the ship hit an iceberg in the North Atlantic Ocean in 1912. To dig deeper into the issue:

Research the *Titanic* disaster. What other ships were able to receive *Titanic*'s radio messages? What was the first ship to arrive on the scene of the accident? About how many lives were likely saved because this ship was able to pick up survivors?

Summary

As wireless equipment improved, radio waves could be sent over longer and longer distances.

Further Inquiry

Radio waves can be sent and received. Maybe we should ask:

What is two-way radio?

What Is Two-Way Radio?

Most radios that people use today can only receive signals, not send them. Two-way radios are devices that allow people to both send and receive messages. These radios have several special uses.

In some areas of the world, it is impossible or very difficult to communicate by telephone. The technology for telephone communication is lacking in such regions. Two-way radio allows people in these areas to talk to one another. It is also used by airplane pilots. The pilots keep in contact with air traffic controllers at airports to find out when it is safe to take off and land. Police officers, ambulance workers, and firefighters all use two-way radio to stay in contact with one another.

▼ Helicopter pilots use two-way radio to communicate with people on the ground.

▲ Using two-way radios, hikers on different parts of a trail can talk to one another.

Truck drivers and others sometimes use a type of two-way radio called CB radio to talk to other drivers. CB stands for citizen's band. CB radio allows truckers to warn other drivers of weather or road problems. It is also a way to help pass the time during long trips. CB radio can be used only over very short distances.

Amateur radios are another way to communicate. They allow people to pick up and send radio signals around the world. Many people use amateur radios as a hobby. These radios also allow people to communicate during emergencies, when telephones are not working.

Your Challenge!

There are several types of two-way radios. To dig deeper into the issue:

Research the devices called walkie-talkies. When were they first developed? How are they used today? List some things users can and cannot do with walkie-talkies compared to other two-way radios.

Summary

Two-way radios are similar in many ways to regular radios. A major difference is that they allow people to both send and receive messages.

Further Inquiry

Spoken messages can be sent by two-way radio, but that is not the only way people communicate by voice over distances. Maybe we should ask:

How do landline telephones work?

How Do Landline Telephones Work?

Telephones allow people to talk to each other over long distances. Landline phones use wires to carry these messages. Many homes and offices have landline phones.

Often, people hold a part of the phone called the handset when using a landline telephone. The handset has a mouthpiece and an earpiece. People speak into the mouthpiece and listen to the earpiece.

The sound waves from a person's voice are converted into electric current by a device in the mouthpiece called a transmitter. A carbon transmitter sends signals using a diaphragm, or thin metal disk, and a cup of carbon grains. The sound waves make the diaphragm vibrate. As it vibrates, it puts pressure on the carbon grains. Electric current flows through the grains. The current copies the pattern of vibrations. It becomes a copy of the speaker's sound waves that travels through wires to another telephone.

❯ The equipment used by telephone companies can send thousands of calls to the correct destination at the same time.

The handset's earpiece has a device called a receiver that changes the electric current back into sound. The receiver has a diaphragm that is surrounded by a ring-shaped permanent magnet. Another magnet, which is an electromagnet, is attached to the diaphragm. Electricity from the sender's message makes the electromagnet pull the diaphragm in different directions from the permanent magnet. This causes the diaphragm to vibrate. The vibration creates sound waves that are the same as those of the sender's voice.

Most landline telephones are connected by a **cable** to a nearby telephone exchange. Exchanges have equipment that directs each call to the proper destination. A call to another country is first sent to an international exchange. Telephone cables are buried under the ocean floor to connect continents.

Digging Deeper

Your Challenge!

Telephone technology may seem complex, but it does not have to be. To dig deeper into the issue:

Make your own simple "telephone." First, poke a small hole through the bottoms of two clean, empty cans. Thread a string through the holes, and knot each end of the string to secure it inside each can. Give one can to a friend. Pull the string tight and then talk and listen to each other. Why does this device work? Research the answer.

Summary

Landline telephones convert sound waves into electric current.

Further Inquiry

Landline telephones used to be the only telephones, but that is not the case today. Maybe we should ask:

How do cellular telephones work?

How Do Cellular Telephones Work?

Cellular telephones are often called cell phones or mobile phones. They are not connected to telephone exchanges by wires or cables. Cell phones are a combination of a telephone and a two-way radio.

Like most telephones, a cell phone changes voices into electric current. Instead of sending the electrical signals along cables, cell phones send them on radio waves that travel through the air. These waves are picked up by **antennas** on a receiving and transmitting station.

ᐯ Many cell phones have cameras, and people often enjoy taking pictures of themselves, called selfies.

▲ The towers holding equipment that sends and receives cell phone calls are sometimes made to look like trees, so that they will blend into their surroundings.

Receiving and transmitting stations are spread out across a region. Each receives radio signals sent out from mobile phones in a small area called a cell. Stations in different cells are all linked to a central computer. If a person moves from one cell to another while using a mobile phone, the computer automatically switches the call to the nearest receiving and transmitting station.

A smartphone is a type of cell phone that also has a computer built into it. The computer connects the device to the **Internet**. Information is carried between the phone and the Internet using radio waves. Often, a smartphone reaches the Internet using the same receiving and transmitting stations that are used for cell phone calls. Many people use "apps," short for *applications*, with their smartphones to do such things as play games and **download** music from a website.

Your Challenge!

The cells in a region often overlap one another to prevent calls from being lost while people are on the go. To dig deeper into the issue:

Contact the company that provides your family's cell phone service, or look at the company's website. Find a map of the company's cell network in your region. Are there any places where you are not able to use your family's cell phones?

Summary

Cellular phones use a combination of radio and telephone technology. They send and receive signals throughout a cell network, which is linked by a central computer.

Further Inquiry

There are many other ways in which technology helps people communicate. Maybe we should ask:

How do fax machines and scanners work?

How Do Fax Machines and Scanners Work?

Fax machines send and receive written words and pictures through telephone lines. Fax is short for *facsimile*, which means "copy." A fax machine sends an exact copy of what is on a piece of paper to another fax machine. This means that handwriting, illustrations, and even photographs can be sent by fax.

Both the sender and the receiver must have a fax machine or a computer with fax **software**. A fax machine divides a page into thousands of tiny squares. Each square is turned into a unique sound signal, depending on the darkness or lightness of the square. When the signals reach the receiving fax machine, they are turned back into squares. The fax machine then prints out a copy of what the original page looked like. Sending a fax is as quick as making a phone call.

Scanners also make a copy of the words and pictures on a page. A scanner uses light to reflect an image of the page into the machine. A **digital** copy of the page is made from that reflection. This digital copy, or scan, can then be printed, viewed, and saved on a computer. It can also be emailed or faxed.

❯ Some fax machines can print 20 or more pages in one minute.

Digging Deeper

Your Challenge!

Some scanners can make very realistic copies. To dig deeper into the issue:

Some criminals have used scanners to make counterfeit, or fake, copies of paper money. Using the website of the U.S. Mint and other sources, research what steps governments are taking to stop counterfeiting. List several features of U.S. paper money that make the bills harder to copy.

Summary

Fax machines and scanners make copies of documents that can be sent to people using telephone lines and computers.

Further Inquiry

With technology constantly improving the way we communicate, maybe we should ask:

How have satellites improved communication?

How Have Satellites Improved Communication?

It is sometimes difficult to send radio signals over long distances. Radio waves can have problems traveling over hills and mountains. The waves cannot curve around Earth's surface. Some radio waves can bounce off the layer of the atmosphere called the ionosphere and be reflected back to Earth. However, not all wavelengths are reflected. In addition, several conditions can prevent radio waves from bouncing off the ionosphere, including time of day.

Bouncing radio waves off communication satellites is a much more reliable way to send signals around the world. Communication satellites are shot into space using rockets. They then orbit Earth, pick up radio waves transmitted from one location, and send them back to other locations on the planet.

The first communication satellite was sent into space in 1960. This satellite, called Echo I, was shaped like a huge metal ball. It sent weak signals back to Earth.

A more powerful communication satellite, Telstar, was sent into orbit in 1962. Telstar worked very well and communicated with transmitting and receiving stations in the United States and Great Britain. Today, hundreds of satellites orbit Earth. They allow clear, quick communication all over the world of telephone, television, and radio signals, as well as information from Internet sites.

Aqua

Terra

Aura

Digging Deeper

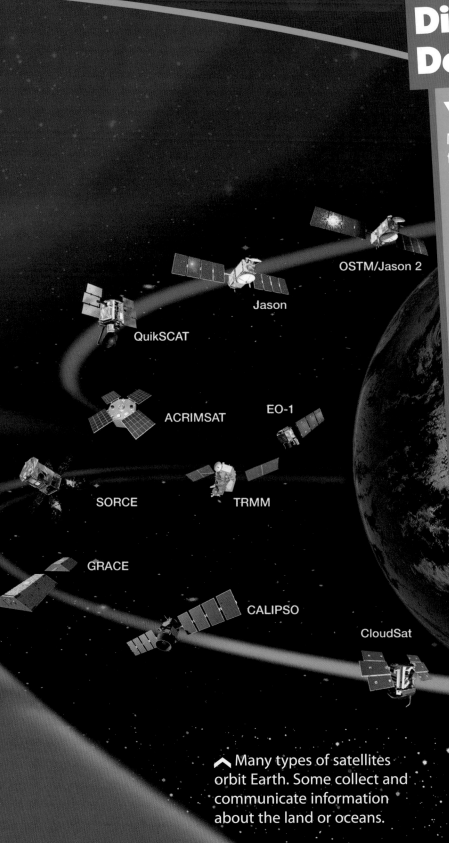

QuikSCAT

Jason

OSTM/Jason 2

ACRIMSAT

EO-1

SORCE

TRMM

GRACE

CALIPSO

CloudSat

⌃ Many types of satellites orbit Earth. Some collect and communicate information about the land or oceans.

Your Challenge!

Millions of people benefit from satellite communication in their daily lives. To dig deeper into the issue:

Make a list of ways your family used satellite communication during one week. The list might include such things as phone calls with friends or relatives who were far away or television broadcasts of sports or news events taking place around the world.

Summary

Communication satellites pick up radio waves from Earth and send them back to distant locations around the planet.

Further Inquiry

Satellites bring television broadcasts from around the world into people's homes. Maybe we should ask:

How does television work?

How Does Television Work?

Television is similar to radio, but it uses pictures as well as sounds to communicate. A television signal starts when light from the scene being shot enters the TV camera. The camera changes the light into electric signals. A microphone picks up the sound and changes sound waves into electric signals at the same time. These signals are sent into the air using radio waves. A receiver in a home television set makes sense of the signals. The receiver changes them back into copies of the light and sound waves recorded by the camera and microphone.

▼ Since the late 1990s, some television signals have been sent using a technology called high definition, or HD, which makes pictures look sharper. TVs with even better-quality, called Ultra HD or UHD, are becoming available.

^ The number of televisions in U.S. homes rose from 6,000 in 1946 to 12 million just five years later.

Television was invented in the 1920s. However, regular television broadcasts, by the networks NBC and CBS, did not start until the late 1940s. Early televisions were large, but they had small screens. Many screens were only about 10 inches (25 centimeters) square. Only black-and-white images were available, and they were not very clear. As a result, people often sat just a few feet (meters) from the TV screen to watch a program. Color television was invented in the 1960s. Color television signals are broken down into red, green, and blue light. These signals are changed back to the original colors in home television sets.

Digging Deeper

Your Challenge!

Millions of people enjoy watching sports on television. To dig deeper into the issue:

The first sports event broadcast on television was a baseball game. Research when this took place and about how many people watched the broadcast. How does the number of viewers compare with the number of people who watch a baseball World Series game today?

Summary

Television works by turning sound and pictures into electrical signals. These are sent to a receiver in a television set, where they are turned back into sound and pictures.

Further Inquiry

Television technology has come a long way since the earliest broadcasts. Maybe we should ask:

What are cable, satellite, and Internet television?

What Are Cable, Satellite, and Internet Television?

All television sets used to need antennas to receive television signals. TV sets were made with antennas on top. Tall buildings or other objects could make it hard for antennas to pick up radio waves. Many homes and other buildings had television antennas on their roofs to pick up TV signals. A rooftop antenna was connected by a wire to the TV set. Any type of antenna had to be close to a local television station in order to pick up signals. Cable television and satellite television allow people to receive signals from much farther away.

Cable television companies send TV signals to people's homes using cables, rather than through the air. Large amounts of information can be sent through these cables. This gives TV viewers a choice of hundreds of channels, and signals cannot be blocked by buildings.

At first, all companies used cables made of metal wires. Today, some companies use fiber-optic cables. These cables are made of thin strands of glass, and they can carry even more information than metal cables. Electric signals are changed to pulses of light to be carried over fiber-optic cables.

People who own a satellite dish can get television signals from around the world without using a cable company. A satellite dish is a special type of antenna that receives signals directly from satellites in space. Satellite TV companies collect programs from around the world and send these programs to their customers using satellites.

Some Internet sites now provide television programs, movies, and other videos to people around the world. Depending on the site, programs may or may not be free. Sometimes, programs may be downloaded and saved onto a computer. Other programs may be available through **streaming**. People can watch these programs on a home computer, laptop computer, **tablet**, or smartphone.

❯ Satellite dishes may be very useful in areas where there are no cables to carry TV programs.

Digging Deeper

Your Challenge!

There are many options for watching television. To dig deeper into the issue:

Take a survey of family members, friends, and classmates. Record how many of them use cable TV, satellite TV, or Internet streaming to watch television programs. Make a chart to show your results.

Summary

Many televisions today receive signals through metal or fiber-optic cables. Others receive signals sent from satellites.

Further Inquiry

Many people are also using their computers to watch television programs. Maybe we should ask:

How do computers talk to one another?

How Do Computers Talk to One Another?

In order for people to communicate using computers, the machines must be linked to each other through a common network. A computer network is a connection between two or more computers. It allows digital information to be sent quickly from one computer to many others. Through a network, a computer can send messages to other computers almost anywhere in the world.

There are two main types of computer networks. They are local area networks (LANs) and wide area networks (WANs). Computers in one location, such as a business office or a home, can be connected in a LAN. The LAN may also include other devices, such as a printer. Sometimes, the devices are connected using metal or fiber-optic cables. Some LANs have wireless connections, in which signals are sent between computers using electromagnetic waves.

Computers in different buildings or even different countries can be linked to form a WAN. Connections in a WAN may also use cables or electromagnetic waves sent through the air. Some WANs use satellites to send signals over long distances.

> In wireless local area networks, a device called a router is used to connect computers, printers, and scanners to the network.

▲ A computer may be connected to a network by plugging a cable into a slot in the computer called a port.

Router

Your Challenge!

Computers must be connected through a common network to communicate with one another. To dig deeper into the issue:

Investigate whether there is a LAN in your school, a place where a parent works, or your home. Ask a parent or teacher for help. Make a map to show the devices that are connected in the LAN. Are these devices connected by cables or wirelessly?

Summary

A computer network allows messages to be sent quickly from one computer to many others. The other computers may be in the same room or across the globe.

Further Inquiry

With computers able to communicate over long distances, maybe we should ask:

How does the Internet work?

How Does the Internet Work?

The Internet is often called the largest computer network in the world. It is made up of many smaller networks. These smaller networks belong to government agencies, universities, businesses, and other groups or individuals. People around the world are connected to the Internet through their computers and smartphones.

The Internet began in 1969. At first, it was used only by the United States military. Soon, it was also used by businesses and large organizations to send information and messages. Most people did not use the Internet at first because very few people had a computer at home. In the 1980s, small, inexpensive personal computers, or PCs, were developed. This meant that more people could afford a computer. They could also connect to the Internet.

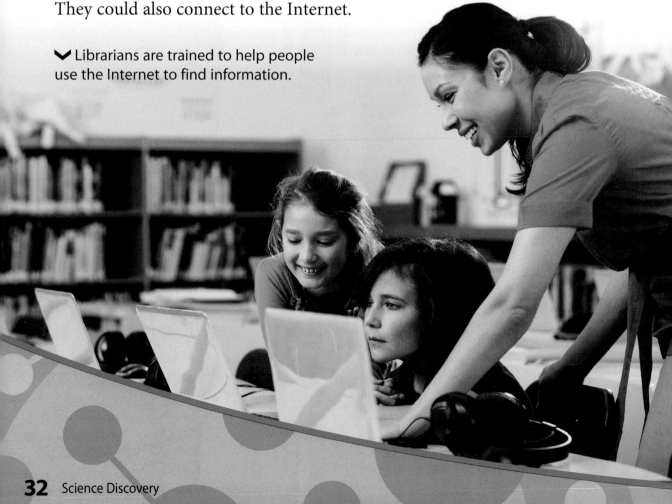

❯ Librarians are trained to help people use the Internet to find information.

△ Many people use the Internet to look for bargains when shopping.

In the past, most people connected to the Internet using telephone lines. A device called a modem changed signals carried by phone lines into digital information that a computer can use. Today, many people have what is called broadband or high-speed access to the Internet. They receive information through cables that can carry many more words, sounds, and pictures each second than phone lines could. Broadband Internet access may be offered by companies that also provide cable television service.

In many public places and in some homes, people use Wi-Fi to access the Internet. A Wi-Fi system is a wireless LAN that uses radio waves to send information. Many smartphones and tablets can connect to the Internet using a cellular telephone network or a Wi-Fi network if one is available.

Your Challenge!

About 100 million people in the United States do not have access to a broadband connection to the Internet. To dig deeper into the issue:

Research the U.S. government's National Broadband Plan to give all Americans access to high-speed Internet service by the year 2020. How will the plan achieve this goal? What are some of the benefits that can come from greater broadband access?

Summary

The Internet did not exist until the late 1960s. Today, it is the world's largest computer network.

Further Inquiry

People around the world use the Internet daily to access the World Wide Web. Maybe we should ask:

What is the World Wide Web?

What Is the World Wide Web?

The World Wide Web, or the web, is a collection of sites containing information that are reached using the Internet. Each website has one or more web pages. Web pages contain information in many forms, including words, pictures, sounds, and video. They present information in a way that is easy for people to see and use.

❯ Devices of all sizes are used to view web pages.

▲ The Internet has about 125 trillion web pages. Some pages are available to the public, and some are not.

Your Challenge!

People's lives have changed a great deal since the World Wide Web became widely used in the 1990s. To dig deeper into the issue:

Talk to a parent, teacher, or other adult who grew up without the web. List several ways that the World Wide Web has changed the way this person communicates, learns, works, and has fun?

Summary

The World Wide Web is made up of billions of web pages.

Further Inquiry

With technology offering so many communication options, maybe we should ask:

How do email and text messaging work?

Websites use hyperlinks to help people travel from one web page to another. Hyperlinks are pictures or words that are connected to other sites or documents on the web. Linked words are called hypertext. People can click on a hyperlink using a computer's **cursor** or tap the hyperlink on a tablet or smartphone screen. When they click or tap, they are taken to a different web page.

To use the World Wide Web, people need a computer or smartphone with an Internet connection and a browser. A browser is a computer program that helps people move around the web. Search engines, or programs that help people find specific web pages, allow users to search for websites that have information on any chosen subject.

How Do Email and Text Messaging Work?

Email, which is short for *electronic mail*, is a way of sending messages and information over the Internet. Messages can include words and pictures. Other things can be attached to an email message. These attachments may include documents with written information, pictures, and videos. Once a message is sent, it takes only seconds to reach another computer anywhere in the world.

To send and receive email, people need a computer or smartphone with email software and access to the Internet. When a person sends an email message, his or her computer directs it to another computer called a mail server. That computer then sends the message to the proper email address. The message gets stored in the receiver's electronic mailbox until he or she opens it.

Text messaging is a common way to get a brief message to someone. Its official name is SMS, which stands for *short message service*. People type a message into the SMS program on their cell phones. Once the message is sent, it is received a short time later on another person's cell phone. A text message travels in the same way as a cell phone call. The difference is that it is text, not sound, that is converted into electrical signals carried on radio waves. Text messaging programs in many phones can also be used to send pictures and videos.

▼ Many people use messaging programs to send a photo to friends as soon as they take it.

Digging Deeper

Your Challenge!

Email and text messaging are two fast ways to communicate with people. To dig deeper into the issue:

Email and text messaging affect the way people write. To type a text message faster, many people use abbreviations instead of writing out the words, such as "BTW" instead of "by the way." Research and make a list of several other commonly used abbreviations. Compare the number of letters in each abbreviation to the number in the written-out words.

Summary

Email and SMS are easy ways to get messages to people anywhere in a short amount of time.

Further Inquiry

Writing messages is just one way people communicate. Maybe we should ask:

What are other ways people communicate?

What Are Other Ways People Communicate?

When the web first came into widespread use, it offered pages for people to view and read. Later, the web became more interactive. This means that people could provide information as well as see it. The term *Web 2.0* has been used to describe this interactive phase of the web's development. Web users are now able to create and share their own content.

⌄ Band members in different locations can play music together using the Internet.

▲ Online video games can be played alone or with people anywhere in the world.

Millions of people use social media websites, such as Facebook, Instagram, and Snapchat, to share messages and pictures with friends. Many people have started their own blogs. A blog is a website in which the writer shares his or her own opinions and experiences. Some blogs have become very popular. Millions of people read blogs and are able to add their own comments on the site about what the writer has said.

A type of site where people can create content together is called a wiki. Many people in different locations can write on one shared site. The Internet encyclopedia Wikipedia is an example of a wiki. However, readers of wikis need to be careful. Since many people can add information to a wiki, it may be hard for a reader to know whether the content is fair and accurate.

Millions of people use the web to play video games. Playing other games, such as chess, on the Internet has also become popular. Some people use the web to take college courses without ever going to a school building.

How Is Information Sent in an Emergency?

When an emergency happens, fast and clear communication helps ensure safety. Emergency communication systems allow people to report an incident and get responders to the scene. Emergency notification systems inform the public of an emergency.

The phone number 9-1-1 is used in the United States to report emergencies. When a person calls 9-1-1 from a landline phone, the call is routed through the phone wires to a local 9-1-1 switch. This device quickly sends the call to the Public Safety Answering Point located nearest to where the call was placed. The phone service also sends an Automatic Number Identification (ANI) signal. The ANI contains the address from which the call was made.

⌄ About ten minutes before arriving at a hospital, an ambulance crew radios ahead to say a patient is coming and to provide information about the patient's condition.

▲ The digits 9-1-1 were selected for emergency calls in part because the numbers are easy to find on a telephone in the dark.

When the call is answered in a 9-1-1 call center, the caller's telephone number and address appear on a computer screen. The operator confirms the caller's location. He or she then asks a series of questions about the emergency and types the information into a computer. A dispatcher reads the information and decides what types of emergency responders are needed. These responders may be firefighters, police officers, or emergency medical technicians. The dispatcher contacts the emergency responders on a two-way radio system, and help is on the way.

If a cell phone is used to call 9-1-1, there is no ANI. The 9-1-1 call center may be able to determine the caller's location using the phone's **global positioning system** (GPS). Many cell phones contain GPS technology.

In an emergency such as an approaching storm or wildfire, officials use several forms of communication to warn the public. Some cities and states offer emergency contact registries. People can provide their address, phone number, and email address. They will then receive advance warning of an emergency in their area.

Digging Deeper

Your Challenge!

Emergency responders are specially trained to use communication equipment to receive and share information. To dig deeper into the issue:

With the help of a parent or teacher, try to arrange a visit to a local police station, fire station, or ambulance corps. Ask for a demonstration of communication equipment used to find out about and respond to emergencies.

Summary

Emergency systems depend on telephone, computer, radio, and satellite technology.

Further Inquiry

Fully understanding communication technology has involved asking many questions and researching many issues. Taking all we have learned, maybe we finally can answer:

What is communication?

Putting It All Together

Throughout history, people have always wanted to communicate with one another. Technology has helped them do that more quickly and easily. The printing press first allowed people to share written words and pictures with many readers. The discovery of electricity and the invention of the telegraph and telephone allowed people to connect across great distances. Satellites in space bring pictures and sound from all over the world to people's homes, cars, and mobile phones. Today's computer technology allows people to share ideas and messages in the blink of an eye.

Where People Fit In

Communication technology has changed very quickly in recent years. What has not changed is the importance of the content of messages and information. Clearly written communication helps other people understand the message being sent. It is also as important as ever that information being communicated is accurate. In addition, communication should not be hurtful to anyone receiving a message.

ᐁ The number of different devices people use for communication today is much greater than in the past.

Communication Careers

Web Developer and Webmaster

Web developers create web pages for companies or organizations. The web developer makes sure the website includes all the information and features, such as photos and videos, that the company wants to share with the public. Webmasters are the people who maintain web pages. The webmaster makes sure a website is running smoothly. The webmaster also makes changes to the site as needed to keep all of the information up-to-date. In addition, he or she makes sure that all emails or other messages sent to the website are answered. Many web developers and webmasters have college degrees in computer science or have taken computer courses at a community college.

Electronics Technician

Electronics technicians build, install, or repair electrical equipment used for communicating. Electronics technicians work with equipment such as telephones, televisions, and computer networks. If telephone systems are not working, technicians repair the problem. They may repair problems at telephone exchanges. Technicians also repair the cables that connect computers, fax machines, and other electronic equipment. Today's technology has created more jobs for electronics technicians. The popularity of television, telephones, and the Internet means that many technicians are needed in the communication industry. Often, electronics technicians have taken training courses at a technical school or community college.

Young Scientists at Work

You can make a simple printing press at home to learn about how a printing press works.

Materials

- A rubber eraser
- A knife to cut the eraser
- Glue
- Two flat pieces of wood or stiff cardboard
- Ink
- Paper

Instructions

1. Ask an adult to help you cut the eraser into long, thin strips.

2. Glue the strips onto one of the wood boards or pieces of cardboard to shape a word or words. The words and letters must all be backward.

3. Carefully use a small paintbrush or ink pad to apply ink to the rubber letters pasted on the first board.

4. Place the paper over your words.

5. Put the second board over the paper.

6. Press down evenly on the top board for several seconds.

7. Remove the top board, and then carefully remove the paper. Your word or words should now be printed on the paper.

Observations

Using your printer, make 12 copies of the message you created. If you need to, add more ink to the rubber strips. Time how long it takes to print the 12 copies.

Then, write the same message 12 times using a pen or pencil. Time how long that takes.

Which method made the 12 copies faster?

Quiz

How often do you use the different types of communications equipment discussed in this book? Many people use landlines or cellular telephones. Most people have televisions at home and use computers at home, at school, or at work. You may not realize just how often you use communications devices.

How many hours a week do you spend using the Internet at home and at school?

Do you have an email address? Which do you use more often, email or text messaging?

Where do you and your family get your news? How many different forms of communication do you use to keep up on current events?

How many times do you use a landline telephone or cell phone every day? Which type of phone are you more likely to use?

Key Words

antennas: devices, often made of metal and shaped like rods, that receive and send radio signals

cable: wires that are twisted together

cursor: a pointer on a computer screen

digital: a system, often used by computers, of storing pictures, sounds, and information as a series of numbers

download: to copy sounds, pictures, or information onto one's own computer

electromagnets: pieces of metal that become magnetic when electricity passes through them or near them

electronic: using electrical signals

global positioning system: a system that determines location based on communication between a GPS-enabled device and satellites

hardware: pieces of equipment or major parts of devices such as computers and other technology items

internet: a communication network that connects computers around the world

papyrus: an ancient writing material made from plants

satellites: objects that orbit, or circle around, another object, such as human-made weather satellites that orbit Earth

smartphone: a cellular telephone that also can be used for email, reaching the Internet, making purchases, and other types of communication

software: computer programs that allow people to do specific tasks

streaming: sending pictures and sounds continuously to a computer or to another device for immediate viewing and listening

tablet: a small, easy-to-carry computer used mostly for viewing websites, sending and receiving email, taking and sending pictures, and reading ebooks

Index

Log on to www.av2books.com

AV[2] by Weigl brings you media enhanced books that support active learning. Go to www.av2books.com, and enter the special code found on page 2 of this book. You will gain access to enriched and enhanced content that supplements and complements this book. Content includes video, audio, weblinks, quizzes, a slide show, and activities.

AV[2] Online Navigation

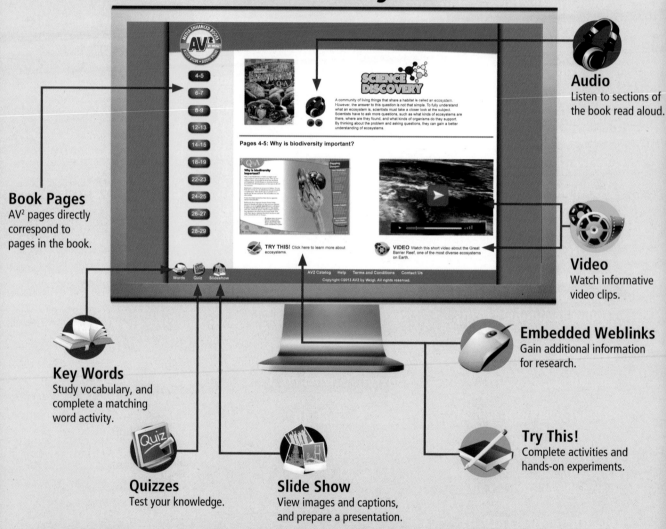

Book Pages
AV[2] pages directly correspond to pages in the book.

Audio
Listen to sections of the book read aloud.

Video
Watch informative video clips.

Key Words
Study vocabulary, and complete a matching word activity.

Embedded Weblinks
Gain additional information for research.

Try This!
Complete activities and hands-on experiments.

Quizzes
Test your knowledge.

Slide Show
View images and captions, and prepare a presentation.

AV[2] was built to bridge the gap between print and digital. We encourage you to tell us what you like and what you want to see in the future.

Sign up to be an AV[2] Ambassador at www.av2books.com/ambassador.